Bringing Forth Soul Consciousness Companion Journal

"Early on in my channeling career while I was experiencing my first multiple sclerosis exacerbation my guide Anubis stated, 'If you learn to fully love only one person, and may it be yourself, you will have exceeded our expectations.'"

— Reverend Annie Bachelder

First Edition
2024

Published 2024

DISCLAIMER
Neither the author nor the publisher assume any responsibility for errors, omissions, or contrary interpretations of the subject matter within.

MEDICAL DISCLAIMER
The information in this book is the result of years of practical experience by the author. This information is not intended as a substitute for the advice provided by your physician or other healthcare professional. Do not use this information for diagnosing or treating a health problem or disease, or prescribing medication or other treatment

ISBN #979-8-9890697-3-6

For more information, visit:
www.anniechannels.com

Table of Contents

Expand to Include

"Expand to Include" is a transformative concept that encourages embracing all aspects of oneself and one's experiences with openness and acceptance. It means broadening your perspective to incorporate not just the light and joyful parts of your journey, but also the challenges, fears, and shadows. "Expand to Include" circumvents the need to defend against, resist, manage, or overcome an experience or memory. It allows you to Expand to Include persons or groups with whom you disagree. By expanding to include everything, you allow for a fuller, richer experience of life. This approach fosters a sense of wholeness and integration, where every part of your being is acknowledged and valued. It's about accepting and loving all aspects of yourself and your journey, knowing that each piece contributes to your growth and spiritual evolution.

Expanding to include welcomes you to approach life's experiences with curiosity and compassion. Instead of resisting or avoiding difficult emotions or situations, you are encouraged to welcome them whole-heartedly as opportunities for learning and growth. This shift in perspective can transform how you interact with the world, fostering greater resilience, empathy, and inner peace. By expanding your capacity to include all that life presents, you cultivate a deeper connection with your true self and the Divine, enabling you to navigate your path with grace and authenticity.

1

How to Use This Journal

Beautiful Soul,

Welcome to the Akashic Records! We provide this Companion Journal to the channeled book "*Bringing Forth Soul Consciousness, an Akashic Records Guide to Living a Fulfilled Life*" as a useful tool to help you tell yourself what you experienced, learned, discovered, and was revealed to you in each chapter and in each open Akashic Records exploration. All Affirmations, Invocations & Prayers can be found at the end of the book.

Please open your Akashic Records using the Bringing Forth Soul Consciousness Akashic Records Prayer, read or listen to a chapter, then write your responses to the Interactive Questions in this journal. This ensures your experience and your responses to the questions accurately describe and document your Akashic Records explorations. Describe as much as you can as thoroughly as you can. You'll be surprised when you reread your notes at how accurate and far reaching the simplest of messages can be.

The Akashic Records Opening and Closing Prayers are at the end of this book.

Take your time. Enjoy these processes as you get to know and trust your Soul, your Masters, Teachers and Loved Ones, the Akashic Beings of Light, and the Great Creatress (the Divine). Let yourself be a beginner, learning a new skill. Let yourself play. There are no "right answers", only the value of honoring your experiences, your body sensations, sense of knowing, images, words, phrases, and concepts revealed in your Soul's Akashic Records. Practice needn't be perfect.

Ask the Akashic Beings of Light and your Masters, Teachers and Loved Ones for help at anytime, for any reason. Should you have more to write than the initial space allows, you will find blank pages in each chapter upon which to continue. Remember to always close your Records at the end of your writing sessions.

— Akashic Beings of Light

2

Chapter 2
Getting Started, Opening Your Akashic Records

First opening of your Akashic Records. What do you feel physically?

_____

_____

_____

_____

How do you feel emotionally?

_____

_____

_____

_____

What changes are you experiencing in your thoughts?

_____

_____

_____

_____

What can you feel, see, hear, and/or sense about your Soul's Light, your Soul's Love, and Consciousness?

_____

_____

_____

_____

Chapter 2
Getting Started, Opening Your Akashic Records

What do you notice about the presence of the Akashic Beings of Light?

_____

_____

_____

_____

What do you sense about the presence of your Masters, Teachers, and Loved Ones?

_____

_____

_____

_____

Second open records exercise: How do you feel physically, emotionally, mentally, and energetically in your open Akashic Records?

_____

_____

_____

_____

Chapter 2
Getting Started, Opening Your Akashic Records

Write down any questions or feelings you have about this process and at a separate open Akashic Records session ask your Master's Teachers and Loved Ones your questions.

_____

_____

_____

_____

What concerns have arisen?

_____

_____

_____

_____

What questions or issues are you curious about exploring in your Akashic Records?

_____

_____

_____

_____

Ask your Masters, Teachers, and Loved Ones how to develop your relationship with them?

_____

_____

_____

_____

Chapter 2
Getting Started, Opening Your Akashic Records

Chapter 2
Getting Started, Opening Your Akashic Records

Chapter 2
Getting Started, Opening Your Akashic Records

Chapter 2
Getting Started, Opening Your Akashic Records

Chapter 2
Getting Started, Opening Your Akashic Records

Well done! Just fantastic. Did you remember to close your Akashic Records with the Closing Prayer? You have learned a new spiritual practice that lets you discover for yourself your Soul's intentions and purposes. You've had lots of new experiences, deepened your relationship with your Masters, Teachers and Loved Ones, the Akashic Beings of Light, Anubis, and embodied your Soul's Light throughout these spiritual processes. You have begun your ourney into a loving, ongoing, embrace with the Great Creatress (the Divine). Give yourself plenty of validation for your efforts to describe your differing states of consciousness, and for applying yourself thoroughly. Give yourself credit for the courage you've shown as you learned a whole new set of skills. We will see you on the inner planes of your Soul's Consciousness as your journey continues. Like the Akashic Records, we remain at your service and are available in their entirety, at all times, in all places.

— Akashic Beings of Light

Chapter 3
Going Forward in Space and Time

How do you feel when you embody your Soul's Light?

_____

_____

_____

_____

How are you inspired to "float from one moment to another"?

_____

_____

_____

_____

In what areas of your life are you able to release rigid control?

_____

_____

_____

_____

In what areas do you need Divine Assistance with releasing control?

_____

_____

_____

_____

Chapter 3
Going Forward in Space and Time

How do you feel when you allow the Great Creatress to help you?

_____

_____

_____

_____

_____

_____

_____

_____

_____

_____

_____

_____

_____

_____

_____

_____

_____

Chapter 3
Going Forward in Space and Time

Chapter 3
Going Forward in Space and Time

Chapter 3
Going Forward in Space and Time

Bravo! Did you remember to close your Akashic Records with the Closing Prayer? You have learned to embody your Soul's Light, an important activity that you'll use in all areas of your life. You've enriched your connections with your Masters and Akashic Beings of Light, uniting with your Soul. Recognize yourself and your dedication to utilizing the new skills you've acquired. We'll be with you on the inner planes of your Soul. Available always.

— Akashic Beings of Light

Chapter 4
Annie's Introduction to the Light

Describe your introduction to "the Light", to Christ Light, or to perceptible beneficial energy?

_____

_____

_____

_____

What elements do you relate to in this chapter?

_____

_____

_____

_____

What does "the Light" or "Christ Light" feel like to you?

_____

_____

_____

_____

Who opened the doors to "the Light" for you?

_____

_____

_____

_____

Chapter 4
Annie's Introduction to the Light

Chapter 4

Annie's Introduction to the Light

Chapter 4
Annie's Introduction to the Light

Well done! Did you remember to close your Akashic Records with the Closing Prayer? Your new experiences are deepening your relationships with your Masters, Teachers, and Loved Ones and the Akashic Beings of Light. Your practices have led you to link with your Soul. Validate your efforts and bravery in learning new skills. We will see you on your Soul's inner planes. Ever at your service.

— Akashic Beings of Light

Chapter 5
How I Learned to Channel

How do you feel about channeling?

_____

_____

_____

_____

Do you already have a "Spirit Guide" and what is your shared higher purpose?

_____

_____

_____

_____

What questions do you bring to your Guide?

_____

_____

_____

_____

Describe an experience where you felt you were spontaneously channeling?

_____

_____

_____

_____

Chapter 5
How I Learned to Channel

What information came through?

_____

_____

_____

_____

_____

_____

How was it useful, applicable, and life enhancing?

_____

_____

_____

_____

_____

_____

_____

Chapter 5
How I Learned to Channel

Chapter 5
How I Learned to Channel

Chapter 5
How I Learned to Channel

Congratulations! You've had many new experiences and strengthened your bonds with your Masters, Teachers and Loved Ones, and the Akashic Beings of Light, as you become conscious of your Soul. Did you remember to close your Akashic Records with the Closing Prayer? Celebrate your dedication and courage in acquiring new skills. We'll see you in your Soul's inner realms. Always here for you.

— Akashic Beings of Light

Chapter 6
How Healing Transpires in the Akashic Records

How do you feel with your Records open?

_____

_____

_____

_____

Please describe the Light of your Soul.

_____

_____

_____

_____

What do you detect as your Soul's Consciousness?

_____

_____

_____

_____

How are you emotionally and physically affected by your Soul's Consciousness?

_____

_____

_____

_____

Chapter 6
How Healing Transpires in the Akashic Records

What are four Soul qualities you experience with your Akashic Records open?

_____

_____

_____

_____

_____

_____

Please describe your experience of your Soul's linking abilities to the Great Creatress.

_____

_____

_____

_____

_____

_____

_____

Chapter 6
How Healing Transpires in the Akashic Records

Chapter 6
How Healing Transpires in the Akashic Records

Chapter 6
How Healing Transpires in the Akashic Records

Before we acknowledge your hard work, please remember to close your records. Excellent work! You've gained new experiences and deepened your relationships with your Masters, Teachers, and Loved Ones and merged with your Soul. Validate your efforts and bravery in learning new skills. We will meet you on the inner planes of your Soul's consciousness. Ever present for you.

— Akashic Beings of Light

Chapter 7
How the Soul is Constructed

Utilizing the exercise "How to Embody Your Soul's Light", how do you feel when the column of Soul's Light between your 7th and 8th chakras is filled in with Soul Light and frequencies?

_____

_____

_____

_____

In the exercise, what changes for you when you interact with the column of Soul Light between your 7th and 8th chakras?

_____

_____

_____

_____

What Soul quality did you add to the column of Light? Why?

_____

_____

_____

_____

Chapter 7
How the Soul is Constructed

What desired event did you insert into the column of Soul Light?

_____

_____

_____

_____

Describe the embarrassing moment, or the regret, that the Akashic Beings of Light removed through your column of Soul Light. How do you feel now?

_____

_____

_____

_____

Knowing that you and your Soul are divinely designed to be intricately linked, what seems possible in your life now?

_____

_____

_____

_____

Chapter 7
How the Soul is Constructed

Chapter 7
How the Soul is Constructed

Chapter 7
How the Soul is Constructed

Great job! This a very esoteric chapter and we encourage you to reread or listen to it again so that you absorb the information fully. Your new experiences and deepened connections with your Masters, Teachers, and Loved Ones have brought you into closeness with your Soul. Affirm your dedication and the courage you've shown in acquiring new information and skills. We'll meet you in your Soul's inner realms. Always at your service. Remember to close your Akashic Records with the closing prayer.

— Akashic Beings of Light

Chapter 8
Following the Energy

Describe a time when you felt drawn to follow the energy, or fel led by the energy.

_____

_____

_____

_____

Describe three times and three methods you used to ground yourself.

_____

_____

_____

_____

How do you feel about the messages from the Akashic Beings of Light?

_____

_____

_____

_____

Describe your experience of your Spiritual Heart.

_____

_____

_____

_____

Chapter 8
Following the Energy

Chapter 8
Following the Energy

Chapter 8
Following the Energy

Bravo! You've had many new experiences of following the energy, employing your Spiritual Heart, and strengthened your ties with the Akashic Beings of Light and embodied your Soul's Light and Consciousness. Celebrate your dedication and bravery in learning new skills. We'll be with you on the inner planes of your Soul. Ever available to you. Remember to close your records.

— Akashic Beings of Light

Chapter 9
The Development of Soul Consciousness

What do you notice about your state of consciousness as your Soul pours Its Light from the 8th chakra (the Soul chakra) into the space between it and your 7th chakra (the Crown chakra)?

_____

_____

_____

_____

Describe your physical sensations as you completely embody your Soul's Light.

_____

_____

_____

_____

Describe your state of consciousness while embodying your Soul's Light.

_____

_____

_____

_____

Chapter 9
The Development of Soul Consciousness

In what ways has your longing for your Soul's Light and connection moved you forward on your spiritual path?

_____

_____

_____

_____

Describe your sense of the complex set of lines (bar code) in the space between your Soul Chakra and the 7th chakra?

_____

_____

_____

_____

What qualities and colors are present in the bar code?

_____

_____

_____

_____

How does it change under different circumstances?

_____

_____

_____

40

Chapter 9
The Development of Soul Consciousness

Chapter 9
The Development of Soul Consciousness

Chapter 9
The Development of Soul Consciousness

Congratulations! Your journey has deepened your relationship with the Akashic Beings of Light and embodied your Soul's Light and Consciousness. Acknowledge your efforts and bravery in mastering new skills and experiencing different energies. We will see you on the inner planes of your Soul's consciousness. Here for you always. Remember to close your Records.

— Akashic Beings of Light

Chapter 10
Embracing Soul Qualities & the Great Creatress

How do you feel when you read or hear the Great Creatress' message?

_____

_____

_____

_____

What questions arise after taking in this chapter?

_____

_____

_____

_____

What creations are you working on where you can feel Her Divine Presence?

_____

_____

_____

_____

Describe a time when the Light slipped in surreptitiously and you were healed or comforted?

_____

_____

_____

_____

Chapter 10
Embracing Soul Qualities & the Great Creatress

Chapter 10
Embracing Soul Qualities & the Great Creatress

Chapter 10
Embracing Soul Qualities & the Great Creatress

Excellent work! Did you remember to close your Akashic Records with the Closing Prayer? You've enriched your connections with the Great Creatress, your Masters, Teachers, and Loved Ones, and the Akashic Beings of Light. Validate your efforts and bravery in acquiring new skills. We'll meet you on the inner planes of your Soul. Ever present for you.

— Akashic Beings of Light

Chapter 11
Your Spiritual Heart

Please describe your experience of your Spiritual Heart.

_____

_____

_____

_____

Please describe your experience of your Soul surrounded by your Spiritual Heart.

_____

_____

_____

_____

Being specific, what do you notice about the availability of the Great Creatress (the Divine) when you are connected to your Soul and your Spiritual Heart?

_____

_____

_____

_____

What core carrier frequencies do you detect in this chapter?

_____

_____

_____

_____

Chapter 11
Your Spiritual Heart

How do you feel when your read or hear Annie's examples of the Spiritual Heart in action?

_____

_____

_____

_____

_____

_____

What questions arise after taking in this chapter?

_____

_____

_____

_____

_____

_____

_____

Chapter 11
Your Spiritual Heart

Chapter 11
Your Spiritual Heart

Chapter 11
Your Spiritual Heart

Well done! Thorough descriptions elevate your awareness of what you are receiving in your Records and help you validate your own experiences. Your new experiences and deepened bonds with the Great Creatress (the Divine), your Masters, Teachers, and Loved Ones, the Akashic Beings of Light, and Anubis. Celebrate your assimilate esoteric information and energy. We'll meet you in your Soul's inner planes as you continue your journey. Always here for you. Remember to close your Akashic Records.

— Akashic Beings of Light

Chapter 12
Masterful Manifesting

Please describe your experience of the first layer of recipients of the connective lines of Light.

_____

_____

_____

_____

How do you feel as you project Light from your Spiritual Heart Center?

_____

_____

_____

_____

What did you experience when projecting lines of Light from your Spiritual Heart to the second layer of recipients?

_____

_____

_____

_____

Describe your experience with the third layer.

_____

_____

_____

_____

Chapter 12
Masterful Manifesting

Was the Light different at different send points?

_____

_____

_____

_____

Please describe your experience as you received Light coming back to you from your intended recipients.

_____

_____

_____

_____

How did you feel when you balanced sending Light from your Spiritual Heart center with receiving Light from your intended recipients?

_____

_____

_____

_____

Chapter 12
Masterful Manifesting

Chapter 12
Masterful Manifesting

Chapter 12
Masterful Manifesting

Bravo! You've learned a whole new way to lovingly manifest on the energy planes using your Spiritual Heart as the connecting link. You've enriched your relationship with your Masters, Teachers, and Loved Ones, and Akashic Beings of Light. Recognize your dedication and the new skills you've acquired. Observe as the results of your Masterful Manifesting arrive over time in your outer reality. Offer gratitude for Divine assistance. We'll be with you on the inner planes of your Soul. Available always. Did you remember to close your Akashic Records with the Closing Prayer?

— Akashic Beings of Light

Chapter 13
Feeling Your Soul's Light in Your Body

Activate your Spiritual Heart. Claim your Soul. Now describe how you feel.

_____

_____

_____

_____

You and your Soul belong together. Describe your experience of belonging.

_____

_____

_____

_____

You can see through the eyes of your Soul. What do you see?

_____

_____

_____

_____

You can love through the Spiritual Heart, the heart of your Soul. How does that feel in your body?

_____

_____

_____

_____

Chapter 13
Feeling Your Soul's Light in Your Body

You are supported by your Soul. As you take in this Divine knowing, what softens?

_____

_____

_____

_____

_____

_____

You are inspired by your Soul. What becomes possible? What options open up for you? Do you detect new solutions coming unto your awareness?

_____

_____

_____

_____

_____

_____

Chapter 13
Feeling Your Soul's Light in Your Body

Chapter 13
Feeling Your Soul's Light in Your Body

Chapter 13
Feeling Your Soul's Light in Your Body

Did you remember to close your Akashic Records with the Closing Prayer?

Well done! Your experiences have deepened relationships with your Akashic Masters, Teachers, and Loved Ones and the Akashic Beings of Light. You to embody your Soul via its Light easily now. Validate your efforts and bravery in learning new skills. We will see you on your Soul's inner planes. Ever at your service.

— Akashic Beings of Light

Chapter 14
Embodiment of Soul's Light & Consciousness

How do you envision yourself exercising these potent freedoms?

_____

_____

_____

_____

What effects ripple out from your actions and decisions?

_____

_____

_____

_____

What new ideas arise in your wily unpredictable human mind and spirit?

_____

_____

_____

_____

Describe how creative and adventurous do you envision being in your co-creations with the Divine Designer?

_____

_____

_____

_____

Chapter 14
Embodiment of Soul's Light & Consciousness

Describe three outlandish requests for help and inspiration while you pray to the Great Creatress (the Divine) for assistance.

_____

_____

_____

_____

How willing can you now be to being redirected?

_____

_____

_____

_____

What happens when you ask the Great Creatress to take over and provide a new opportunity to expand, to gingerly place your consciousness in a new framework, so that many are led to experience the uncharted territory ahead?

_____

_____

_____

_____

Describe how much more adaptable you are when embodying your Soul's Light.

_____

_____

_____

_____

Chapter 14
Embodiment of Soul's Light & Consciousness

Describe your vision and increased creativity while embodying your Soul's Light.

_____

_____

_____

_____

What creative endeavors seem possible with the aid of your Masters, Teachers, and Loved Ones?

_____

_____

_____

_____

What creative endeavors seem possible with the aid of the Great Creatress?

_____

_____

_____

_____

What bursts into possibility when your Angel wings dip into the color pots?

_____

_____

_____

_____

Chapter 14
Embodiment of Soul's Light & Consciousness

Chapter 14
Embodiment of Soul's Light & Consciousness

Chapter 14
Embodiment of Soul's Light & Consciousness

Congratulations! You've had many new experiences and strengthened your bonds with your Masters, Teachers, and Loved Ones, and Embodied Your Soul's Light. Celebrate your dedication and courage in acquiring new skills and freedoms. We'll see you in your Soul's inner realms. Always supporting and loving you and your spiritual and personal growth.

-- Akashic Beings of Light

Chapter 15
Living as Your Soul

With the Soul qualities listed on page 126 of "Bringing Forth Soul Consciousness" in mind, coonsider how your Soul responds to self-judgment?

_____

_____

_____

_____

How does your Soul respond to habitual judgment of others?

_____

_____

_____

_____

How do you, Living as Your Soul, respond to comparison?

_____

_____

_____

_____

Living as Your Soul, what is your experience of worry?

_____

_____

_____

_____

Chapter 15
Living as Your Soul

How do you, Living as Your Soul, respond to your personality's experience of worry?

_____

_____

_____

_____

How would you, Living as Your Soul, exhibit Oneness?

_____

_____

_____

_____

How does your Soul experience Oneness?

_____

_____

_____

_____

How does your Soul demonstrate unity with the Great Creatress?

_____

_____

_____

_____

Chapter 15
Living as Your Soul

How would you, Living as Your Soul, create and manifest?

_____

_____

_____

_____

How does your Soul create and manifest?

_____

_____

_____

_____

How does your Soul prioritize activities?

_____

_____

_____

_____

How does your Soul prioritize states of being?

_____

_____

_____

_____

Chapter 15
Living as Your Soul

Living as Your Soul, what do you envision your life to be like?

_____

_____

_____

_____

Living as Your Soul, how does your mind operate?

_____

_____

_____

_____

Living as Your Soul, what ideas pervade your mind and imaginings?

_____

_____

_____

_____

Living as Your Soul, how do you greet challenges?

_____

_____

_____

_____

Chapter 15
Living as Your Soul

Living as Your Soul, how do you handle problems?

_____

_____

_____

_____

Living as Your Soul, how do you make decisions?

_____

_____

_____

_____

Living as Your Soul, how do you address attachments?

_____

_____

_____

_____

Living as Your Soul, how do you address "control" concerns?

_____

_____

_____

_____

Chapter 15
Living as Your Soul

Describe how you feel when your entire being is animated by your Soul's peace, joy, and acceptance?

_____

_____

_____

_____

_____

_____

Living as Your Soul, how does your Soul contribute to others?

_____

_____

_____

_____

_____

_____

Chapter 15

Living as Your Soul

Chapter 15
Living as Your Soul

Chapter 15

Living as Your Soul

Chapter 15
Living as Your Soul

Chapter 15

Living as Your Soul

Chapter 15
Living as Your Soul

Excellent work! You've gained new experiences Living as Your Soul and begun Living as Your Soul on a practical and applicable experiential level. You may want to repeat this chapter several times, or periodically, as you and your Soul evolve and change. Validate your efforts and bravery in learning new skills. We will meet you on the inner planes of your Soul's consciousness. Ever present for you.

— Akashic Beings of Light

Chapter 16
Soul Consciousness - Next Steps

You have practiced opening your Akashic Records over a dozen times wwhile studying Bringing Forth Soul Consciousness. Describe three benefitical things about your "practice.

_____

_____

_____

_____

Describe an experience of receiving valuable information relating to your next steps while being out in nature.

_____

_____

_____

_____

Describe how your path has gotten easier through Soul Consciousness and connecting with the Divine.

_____

_____

_____

_____

Chapter 16
Soul Consciousness - Next Steps

What spiritual principles have you applied that have amplified and encouraged your spiritual growth?

_____

_____

_____

_____

What Soul Qualities are helping you the most now?

_____

_____

_____

_____

Chapter 16
Soul Consciousness - Next Steps

Chapter 16
Soul Consciousness - Next Steps

Chapter 16
Soul Consciousness - Next Steps

Great job! Your new experiences and deepened connections with your spiritual guides have brought you into intimacy with your Soul. Recognize your dedication and the courage you've shown in acquiring new skills. We'll meet you in your Soul's inner realms. Always at your service.

— Akashic Beings of Light

Chapter 17
Loving Your Fear

Ask your Masters, Teachers, and Loved Ones to show you a past life that involved great fear and leadership.

_____

_____

_____

_____

What helped you face important choices that prompted fear in you?

_____

_____

_____

_____

What gifts have you received from your Soul or the Divine in times of fear?

_____

_____

_____

_____

Chapter 17
Loving Your Fear

Chapter 17
Loving Your Fear

Chapter 17
Loving Your Fear

Bravo! You've had many new experiences and begun a relationship with the Angelic Healing Conclave, learning to Love Your Fear, as you merged with your Soul. Celebrate your dedication and bravery in the practical application of your expanded Soul Consciousness. We'll be with you on the inner planes of your Soul. Ever available to you.

— Akashic Beings of Light

Chapter 18
Healing the Separation

As a reminder, all Affirmations, Invocations & Prayers can be found at the end of this journal. Reviewing the Integrating Soul Prayer, how does your body feel?

_____

_____

_____

_____

Reciting the 'I and My Soul are One' affirmations, how does your body feel?

_____

_____

_____

_____

What do you notice today about your connection with your Soul?

_____

_____

_____

_____

What is different about embodying your Soul's Light compared to when you first began the practice?

_____

_____

_____

Chapter 18
Healing the Separation

How do your thoughts and feelings change when you utilize your Soul as your link with the Divine?

_____

_____

_____

_____

What does "being in a state of wonder" mean to you?

_____

_____

_____

_____

What is your Soul inspiring you to do?

_____

_____

_____

_____

Chapter 18
Healing the Separation

Chapter 18
Healing the Separation

Chapter 18

Healing the Separation

Congratulations! Your journey has deepened your relationship with the Akashic Beings of Light and improved how you merge with your Soul. Acknowledge your efforts and bravery in mastering new skills. We will see you on the inner planes of your Soul's consciousness. Here for you always.

— Akashic Beings of Light

Chapter 19
Etheric Planes of Light, Claiming Your Soul

Describe your sense of knowing, your vision of, or the feeling you have when reading about the Etheric Planes of Light.

_____

_____

_____

_____

At this point in your study of this book how does your Soul's Light and energy feel to you? How has it changed since you began reading this book?

_____

_____

_____

_____

Acknowledge and describe three examples of the effort, the dedication, willingness, and the massive amount of blind faith required to arrive here at this moment?

_____

_____

_____

_____

Chapter 19
Etheric Planes of Light, Claiming Your Soul

Describe a past life or fear that is relevant to you or has caught your attention while reading this chapter.

_____

_____

_____

_____

_____

_____

_____

Chapter 19
Etheric Planes of Light, Claiming Your Soul

Chapter 19
Etheric Planes of Light, Claiming Your Soul

Chapter 19
Etheric Planes of Light, Claiming Your Soul

What an exploration! You've enriched your connection through merging with your Soul. You're investing more trust in your Soul's guidance and wisdom. Validate your efforts and bravery in expanding your Soul Consciousness and acquiring new skills. We'll meet you on the inner planes of your Soul. Ever present for you.

— Akashic Beings of Light

Chapter 20

Alternatives to Worry

What is my resistance regarding _____?

_____

_____

_____

_____

How have I judged myself regarding _____?

_____

_____

_____

_____

How have I compared myself unfairly regarding _____?

_____

_____

_____

_____

What are the hidden obstacles to the resolution of _____?

_____

_____

_____

_____

Chapter 20
Alternatives to Worry

What action can I take today regarding _____?

_____

_____

_____

_____

Embodying Soul's Light and Consciousness, what helps you trust the process that is already under way?

_____

_____

_____

_____

How do you feel when you choose faith in the orderliness of the universe, knowing that the solution to your problem is also already on its way?

_____

_____

_____

_____

Chapter 20
Alternatives to Worry

What information did you receive from your Future Selves regarding a problem that has caused you to worry?

_____

_____

_____

_____

_____

_____

_____

Chapter 20
Alternatives to Worry

Chapter 20
Alternatives to Worry

Chapter 20
Alternatives to Worry

Well done! Your new experiences with the Akashic Transformation Process Master Questions has increased your self-compassion and cleared the way to fully merging with your Soul. Acknowledge and thank yourself for experimenting with new methods and techniques to ameliorate worry. Celebrate your dedication and bravery in learning new skills. We will see you on your Soul's inner planes. Always at your service.

— Akashic Beings of Light

Chapter 21
Transitioning Between States of Consciousness

What happens to your stress level when you recite the Bringing Forth Soul Consciousness Akashic Records Prayer?

_____

_____

_____

_____

How do your nervous and immune systems feel when you bring in your Soul's Light?

_____

_____

_____

_____

Name or describe the different states of consciousness you are currently transitioning between.

_____

_____

_____

_____

Describe your sense of the new neural pathways you are growing to accommodate your expanded Soul Consciousness.

_____

_____

_____

Chapter 21
Transitioning Between States of Consciousness

Chapter 21
Transitioning Between States of Consciousness

Chapter 21
Transitioning Between States of Consciousness

Fantastic work! You've had enriching experiences and deepened bonds with your spiritual guides, merging with your Soul. Celebrate your dedication and bravery in learning new skills. We will meet you on the inner planes of your Soul. Always here for you.

— Akashic Beings of Light

Chapter 22
Going South

Describe a time when you felt yourself "Going South", and rather than run away from your emotions you completely felt your feelings, and naturally came through the experience with a refreshing new perspective.

Next, describe a time when you felt yourself "Going South", and rather than run away from your emotions you completely felt your feelings, and naturally came through the experience with a refreshing new perspective.

_____

_____

_____

_____

Describe a time when you felt yourself "Going South" (kind of going crazy) and you asked for Divine help, and you received the help/clarity/solution you needed.

_____

_____

_____

_____

Describe a time when someone else was "going crazy" and you received deep insight into the inner workings of another human being. What was the insight? How were you changed?

_____

_____

_____

_____

Chapter 22

Going South

Chapter 22
Going South

Chapter 22
Going South

Excellent job! Your new experiences and stronger connections with the Akashic Beings and Anubis have brought you closer to your Soul. Recognize your efforts and courage in acquiring new skills. We will be with you in your Soul's inner realms. Ever at your service.

— Akashic Beings of Light

Chapter 23
Anubis Speaks: Healing Past Lives

Set a timer. Embodying your Soul's Light and Consciousness, practice letting your thoughts and judgments arise and dissipate for three minutes.

_____

_____

_____

_____

Ask your Soul or Masters, Teachers, and Loved Ones, "Is what I am thinking and/or feeling sourced in mass consciousness or my consciousness?

_____

_____

_____

_____

Chapter 23
Anubis Speaks: Healing Past Lives

What identifies certain thoughts as mass consciousness?

_____

_____

_____

_____

_____

_____

_____

What distinguishes thoughts that are actually yours?

_____

_____

_____

_____

_____

_____

_____

Chapter 23
Anubis Speaks: Healing Past Lives

Ask your Masters, Teachers, and Loved Ones to show you how to merge your self-will with the Great Creatress' Will. Note how this looks, feels, and changes your energy.

_____

_____

_____

_____

_____

_____

Ask your soul or Masters, Teachers, and Loved Ones to show you how to surrender to the Great Creatress' love and care. Note how that looks, feels and changes your energy.

_____

_____

_____

_____

_____

_____

Chapter 23
Anubis Speaks: Healing Past Lives

Chapter 23

Anubis Speaks: Healing Past Lives

Chapter 23

Anubis Speaks: Healing Past Lives

Chapter 23
Anubis Speaks: Healing Past Lives

Great practice in your Akashic Records! You've deepened your relationship with Anubis, the Great Creatress (the Divine) and your Masters, Teachers, and Loved Ones. You've learned a lot about merging your self will with Divine Will. Validate your dedication and courage in learning so that you can view and know about your past lives. We'll see you on your Soul's inner planes. Always here for you.

— Akashic Beings of Light

Chapter 24
Writing Your Soul's Divine Plan, The Akashic Perspective

Describe three physical, emotional, or mental experiences which have been healed in you.

_____

_____

_____

_____

_____

_____

Describe a situation where disappointment has brought you to healing.

_____

_____

_____

_____

_____

_____

Chapter 24
Writing Your Soul's Divine Plan, The Akashic Perspective

Describe a loss or a disappointment that galvanized a Soul purpose in your Life?

_____

_____

_____

_____

_____

_____

_____

"Beneath every instance of resistance is a fear asking to be healed." Describe a personal example of this.

_____

_____

_____

_____

_____

_____

_____

Chapter 24
Writing Your Soul's Divine Plan, The Akashic Perspective

Chapter 24
Writing Your Soul's Divine Plan, The Akashic Perspective

Chapter 24
Writing Your Soul's Divine Plan, The Akashic Perspective

Superb work! Your experiences and connections with the Akashic Beings have enriched your Soul. Celebrate your sense of knowing the ever-revealing details of your Souls plan and your efforts and bravery in learning new skills, including seeing/knowing things in a new way. We are with you on the inner planes of your Soul. Ever available to you.

— Akashic Beings of Light

Chapter 25
Being of Service

Ask your Masters, Teachers, and Loved Ones to show you a past life of service. Describe the details of time, place, circumstances, others involved, and the emotions you are receiving. Ask your Masters, Teachers, and Loved Ones why this is important to developing Soul Consciousness.

_____

_____

_____

_____

_____

_____

_____

Ask your Masters, Teachers, and Loved Ones to show you a past life where you, or someone close to you, exemplified a misunderstanding between servitude and Being of Service. Describe your emotions, body sensations, visions, and sense of knowing. Ask your Masters, Teachers, and Loved Ones why this is important to your Soul Consciousness.

_____

_____

_____

_____

_____

_____

_____

Chapter 25
Being of Service

Now, ask to be shown a life in between physical embodiments, where you were in training with the Angelic Healing Conclave, or Light Beings, or a similar Consciousness group that serves the Great Creatress. Describe the higher purpose of your education with this group, your emotional state, your consciousness, and your sense of knowing about what is revealed.

_____

_____

_____

_____

_____

_____

Describe the higher purpose of your education with this group, your emotional state, your consciousness, and your sense of knowing about what is revealed.

_____

_____

_____

_____

_____

_____

Chapter 25
Being of Service

Chapter 25

Being of Service

Chapter 25
Being of Service

Chapter 25
Being of Service

Outstanding! You've had profound experiences and strengthened your bond with the Akashic Beings, merging with your Soul. You have taken a deep look at the rewards, costs, and manipulative aspects of Being of Service. Continue to release any old pictures and emotions that are associated with the old paradigm. Recognize and praise your dedication and courage in acquiring new skills. We will meet you in your Soul's inner realms. Always here for you.

— Akashic Beings of Light

Chapter 26
A Discussion of Gender

In your daily life, loosely track how many references to gender occur in an hour, or a day. What do you notice?

_____

_____

_____

Describe how the current gender format works for you.

_____

_____

_____

_____

Describe how the current gender format limits you.

_____

_____

_____

_____

What names for the Divine feel right to you? Why?

_____

_____

_____

_____

Chapter 26
A Discussion of Gender

What is needed so that you can forgive centuries of Ancestors for diminishing females?

_____

_____

_____

_____

What is needed so you can forgive much of humanity for assigning Divine and Earthly authority to males?

_____

_____

_____

_____

In what ways are you experiencing the "giant wave of female energy entering the planet"?

_____

_____

_____

_____

Chapter 26
A Discussion of Gender

Chapter 26
A Discussion of Gender

Chapter 26

A Discussion of Gender

Wonderful job! You have taken a different view point on a topic largely left unspoken. Validate your excellent efforts and bravery in perceiving the Akashic perspective. We will see you on the inner planes of your Soul. Ever at your service.

— Akashic Beings of Light

Chapter 27
Prayer

What has your experience of trusting the Divine shown you?

_____

_____

_____

_____

Give an example of trust in the Divine leading to faith.

_____

_____

_____

_____

Ask your Masters, Teachers, and Loved Ones to show you a past life where faith in the Divine resulted in what you, at that time, considered a bad outcome. Describe the circumstances, the time, who was involved, and what was at stake.

_____

_____

_____

_____

_____

_____

_____

Chapter 27
Prayer

Ask your Masters, Teachers, and Loved Ones to help you release any residual energy from that past life. Describe how your Masters, Teachers, and Loved Ones accomplish this and how it feels as your Masters, Teachers, & Loved Ones make this happen.

_____

_____

_____

_____

_____

_____

Ask your Masters, Teachers, and Loved Ones how you can "lighten up" about your spirituality?

_____

_____

_____

_____

_____

_____

_____

Chapter 27

Prayer

Chapter 27
Prayer

Chapter 27
Prayer

Exceptional work! You've enriched your relationship with the Akashic Beings and merged with your Soul. Celebrate your dedication and courage in learning new skills. We'll meet you in your Soul's inner planes. Always here for you.

— Akashic Beings of Light

Chapter 28
Overwhelming Peace

Chapter 28, "Overwhelming Peace," does not contain interactive questions. This chapter is designed to immerse you in a state of deep tranquility and inner calm, preparing you to fully embrace the teachings on Divine Timing that follow. As you transition from the profound prayers of Chapter 27 into Chapter 29, which focuses on awaiting Divine Timing, reflect on the peace and stillness you cultivate here as a foundation for your ongoing spiritual journey.

Next, move to Chapter 29.

Chapter 29
Awaiting Divine Timing

Describe a situation when you were overtaken by self-will and how it worked out.

_____

_____

_____

_____

Describe a time when you were Divinely motivated and inspired to act. How did that situation work out?

_____

_____

_____

_____

What are the hallmarks of your self-will in action?

_____

_____

_____

_____

In what settings are you prone to operating from self-will?

_____

_____

_____

_____

Chapter 29
Awaiting Divine Timing

What are the hallmarks of Divine Will as the operating program in your life?

_____

_____

_____

_____

_____

How are you Awaiting Divine Timing in your life?

_____

_____

_____

_____

_____

_____

Chapter 29
Awaiting Divine Timing

Chapter 29
Awaiting Divine Timing

Chapter 29
Awaiting Divine Timing

Fantastic job! Your experiences and connection with the Divine are teaching you to trust and be patient as you are Awaiting Divine Timing. You've learned more about your self will. Recognize and praise your efforts and your surrenders, and your bravery in acquiring new skills. We will see you on the inner planes of your Soul. Ever present for you.

— Akashic Beings of Light

Chapter 30
Self-Doubt and Disappointment

Describe a situation where you had overwhelming self-doubt. How did that situation work out?

_____

_____

_____

_____

Describe a moment when you misinterpreted your "BS meter" pinging as the red zone as self-doubt.

_____

_____

_____

_____

Describe a deep disappointment and how that affected your self-doubt.

_____

_____

_____

_____

_____

_____

_____

Chapter 30
Self-Doubt and Disappointment

Describe a moment when you were inexorably pulled inward to trust your Soul and/or the Divine.

_____

_____

_____

_____

_____

_____

_____

As you envision a specific change, describe your sense of how Soul Consciousness is influencing you, your feelings, and your action plans.

_____

_____

_____

_____

_____

_____

_____

Chapter 30
Self-Doubt and Disappointment

Chapter 30
Self-Doubt and Disappointment

Chapter 30
Self-Doubt and Disappointment

Superb effort on two highly charged issues! You've perceived from a different point of view and had new experiences empowered by embodying your Soul's Light. Celebrate your dedication to introspection to aid in healing from within. You are absorbing a lot. We are with you on your Soul's inner planes and are always here for you.

— Akashic Beings of Light

Chapter 31
Self-Judgment and Your Inner Critic

Describe how you feel when you "Soften your heart toward your inner critic, soften your heart toward yourself."

_____

_____

_____

_____

In what ways does interacting with your inner critic release the pressure to be perfect?

_____

_____

_____

_____

Describe what shifted when you used your inner critic's activity to remind you to embody your Soul's Light.

_____

_____

_____

_____

Chapter 31
Self-Judgment and Your Inner Critic

What thoughts are you discovering are not your thoughts but are mass consciousness?

_____

_____

_____

_____

_____

_____

What happened when you interacted with your perfectionist or critic as an inner child or inner children?

_____

_____

_____

_____

_____

_____

Chapter 31
Self-Judgment and Your Inner Critic

Chapter 31
Self-Judgment and Your Inner Critic

Chapter 31
Self-Judgment and Your Inner Critic

Outstanding job! Your new perspective and enlarged compassion exemplified by the Akashic Beings of Light has enriched your physical experience and empowered your personality. Recognize your efforts and bravery in acquiring new skills and ways of recognizing and dealing with your self-judgment and inner critic. We will see you in your Soul's inner realms. Ever available to you.

— Akashic Beings of Light

Chapter 32
Beauty

With your Akashic Records open, what do you notice about Beauty in your life?

_____

_____

_____

_____

Describe how you feel when you think about 3 beautiful things or memories?

_____

_____

_____

_____

What are you doing to add Beauty to your life and your surroundings?

_____

_____

_____

_____

Chapter 32
Beauty

How do you feel when you notice the Beauty of your own energy, your connection with your Soul, and the Great Creatress?

_____

_____

_____

_____

_____

_____

_____

Describe 3 beautiful experiences you've had in your Akashic Records.

_____

_____

_____

_____

_____

_____

_____

Chapter 32
Beauty

Chapter 32
Beauty

Chapter 32
Beauty

Well done! Your deepened relationship with beauty, learned to appreciate the lasting effects beauty offers. Beauty has brought you closer to your Soul. Validate your efforts and courage in learning new skills. We'll meet you on your Soul's inner planes. Always here for you.

— Akashic Beings of Light

Chapter 33
By All That is Holy

Following the intense self-reflection and healing work discussed in Chapter 32, "Beauty", you are invited to delve into Chapter 34, which explores the power of past lives through storytelling. However, Chapter 33, "By All That Is Holy," stands as a contemplative interlude without interactive questions. This chapter of the book encourages you to honor and integrate the sacredness of your spiritual experiences, grounding you in a holy reverence that will enrich your understanding of past life influences in the subsequent chapter.

Please continue to Chapter 34.

Chapter 34
The Power of Story, Past Lives

We recommend that you repeat the opening Akashic Prayer in order to perceive the answers to the following interactive questions. Read the instructions all the way through, then close your eyes and receive the answers to one question at a time. Make detailed notes.

Ask the Akashic Beings of Light to show you an informative past life. Assume that what you are perceiving through your sense of knowing, your physical sensations, images, words and phrases, flashes, and intuitions are the correct information. It may help you to start your descriptions with the words, "I get the sense that . . . " or "It feels as if . . . " or "It seems like . . . "

Next, continue to the next page of Chapter 34's interactive questions.

Chapter 34
The Power of Story, Past Lives

Please describe in as much detail as possible the setting, the personalities present, the time in history, the feelings, the actions, and why this past life is being shown to you.

_____

_____

_____

_____

Are you male or female? What tells you this?

_____

_____

_____

Where on Earth are you located?

_____

_____

_____

Chapter 34
The Power of Story, Past Lives

Or are you in between embodiments? Or on another planet or star?

_____

_____

_____

_____

What is your social status?

_____

_____

_____

_____

How are you dressed?

_____

_____

_____

_____

Chapter 34
The Power of Story, Past Lives

Are you inside a building that you can describe?

_____

_____

_____

_____

Describe any other details that flesh out the vision, sensations, and sense of knowing that you have about the past life.

_____

_____

_____

_____

What is the higher purpose of the past life you are being shown?

_____

_____

_____

_____

Chapter 34
The Power of Story, Past Lives

Why is it important?

_____

_____

_____

_____

What were the important lessons learned?

_____

_____

_____

_____

How did you learn them?

_____

_____

_____

_____

Chapter 34
The Power of Story, Past Lives

Keep asking the Akashic Beings of Light, or your Masters, Teachers, and Loved Ones if there is more that you can know about this past life.

_____

_____

_____

_____

Ask your Masters, Teachers, and Loved Ones to help you release everything from the past life that no longer serves you in present time.

_____

_____

_____

_____

Thank your Masters, Teachers, and Loved Ones and the Akashic Beings of Light for their assistance and close your Records.

Chapter 34
The Power of Story, Past Lives

Chapter 34
The Power of Story, Past Lives

Chapter 34

The Power of Story, Past Lives

Chapter 34
The Power of Story, Past Lives

Great job! Your past lives have influenced your current experiences and connections. You have seen and sensed a lot. The Akashic Beings have led you to a greater understanding about the story of certain past lives. Celebrate your dedication and bravery in sensing Akashic energy and seeing through the eyes of tour Soul or of the Guides. We will see you on the inner planes of your Soul. Ever at your service.

— Akashic Beings of Light

Chapter 35
Resistance, Judgment, and Fear, Ancestral Healing

You just did two exercises. What was the issue that involved judging yourself?

_____

_____

_____

_____

How does it feel to be released from judgment jail?

_____

_____

_____

_____

What ancestral fear was presented in the second exercise?

_____

_____

_____

_____

Chapter 35
Resistance, Judgment, and Fear, Ancestral Healing

How are your Ancestors responding to your leadership?

_____

_____

_____

_____

What are you resisting at this time?

_____

_____

_____

_____

How are judgment and fear involved with your resistance?

_____

_____

_____

_____

Chapter 35
Resistance, Judgment, and Fear, Ancestral Healing

Chapter 35
Resistance, Judgment, and Fear, Ancestral Healing

Chapter 35
Resistance, Judgment, and Fear, Ancestral Healing

Congratulations! Your explorations in your Akashic Records have released you from the bondage of fear, judgment, and resistance. Imagine using this on other issues. Your new experiences have increased you trust in your Masters, Teachers, and Loved Ones and brought you into intimacy with your Soul. Recognize your efforts and bravery in acquiring new skills. We will meet you on the inner planes of your Soul. Always here for you. Thank you for remembering to close your Records.

— Akashic Beings of Light

Chapter 36
The Value You Bring to Your Soul

Try phrasing your questions this way: "Please guide me regarding _____."

_____

_____

_____

_____

"What would my Soul have me do about _____?"

_____

_____

_____

_____

"Please show me how to love _____ (body, person, place, thing, group, or habit I am trying to change)."

_____

_____

_____

_____

Chapter 36

The Value You Bring to Your Soul

Why is _____ needed on my Soul's path?

_____

_____

_____

_____

What small step can I take that fulfills my Soul purpose today?

_____

_____

_____

_____

What one thing heals (or strengthens) my body the most, at this time?

_____

_____

_____

_____

Chapter 36
The Value You Bring to Your Soul

How does my Soul envision the next sequence of events within a specified amount of time (day, week, month, year)?

_____

_____

_____

_____

How does forgetting my Divine Origin help me evolve?

_____

_____

_____

_____

How does rediscovering my Divine plan, piece by piece, lifetime by lifetime, help me?

_____

_____

_____

_____

Chapter 36
The Value You Bring to Your Soul

What have I learned by giving away my authority, autonomy, and sovereignty, only to reclaim it over and over again?

_____

_____

_____

_____

Ask your Masters, Teachers and Loved Ones how can I lovingly and effectively operate outside of the limitations of time and space?

_____

_____

_____

_____

Name the gifts, talents, and abilities that are most important to fulfilling my Soul's purposes.

_____

_____

_____

_____

Chapter 36
The Value You Bring to Your Soul

How is my Soul utilizing the above gifts, talents, and abilities to forward Its objectives?

_____

_____

_____

_____

_____

_____

_____

Chapter 36
The Value You Bring to Your Soul

Chapter 36
The Value You Bring to Your Soul

Chapter 36
The Value You Bring to Your Soul

Excellent follow-through! You've enabled yourself to live more fully as your Soul while receiving energy and information from your Akashic Records. Your body and personality are indispensable components of your personal and Soul evolution. Celebrate your dedication and bravery in learning new skills. We'll see you on your Soul's inner planes. Ever present for you.

— Akashic Beings of Light

Chapter 37
Soul Connection

You have been developing and experiencing your Soul's Light and consciousness throughout this book. List three ways your experience has changed over time.

1 _____

_____

_____

_____

_____

2 _____

_____

_____

_____

_____

3 _____

_____

_____

_____

_____

Chapter 37
Soul Connection

Becoming Soul connected allows you to grow into your appointed place within the Divine. Describe how your connection to your Soul and the Great Creatress has deepened.

_____

_____

_____

_____

How does your Soul demonstrate Its unconditional love for you?

_____

_____

_____

_____

How has your Soul's unconditional love for you helped you to unconditionally love yourself?

_____

_____

_____

_____

Chapter 37
Soul Connection

What helps you to repattern your self-concept in the likeness of your Soul and in the likeness of the Great Creatress?

_____

_____

_____

_____

What is your Soul leading you to do now, to further investigate, and to reach for?

_____

_____

_____

_____

In what way(s) are you now being called to serve others?

_____

_____

_____

_____

Chapter 37
Soul Connection

Chapter 37
Soul Connection

Chapter 37
Soul Connection

Excellent personal and spiritual growth! You've fortified your conscious connection with your Soul, your Masters, Teachers and Loved Ones, and with the Akashic Beings of Light. You have a much deeper trust of the Great Creatress (the Divine). Give yourself lots of gold stars for your dedication and bravery in working in the Akashic Records. We'll see you on your Soul's inner planes. Ever present for you. Don't forget to close your Records.

— Akashic Beings of Light

193

Chapter 38
Soul Inspired Action, Creation, and Healing

What are your "true colors" to be unleashed publicly?

_____

_____

_____

_____

_____

_____

Whom are you being drawn to help?

_____

_____

_____

How are you being drawn to serve?

_____

_____

_____

_____

Chapter 38
Soul Inspired Action, Creation, and Healing

How do you see/feel/sense your partnership with your Soul, your Masters, Teachers, and Loved Ones, and the Akashic Beings of Light taking shape?

_____

_____

_____

_____

How are Soul Inspired Action, Creation, and Healing being expressed in you?

_____

_____

_____

_____

The fundamentals of Soul Inspired Action, Creation, and Healing are faith, allowing, trust, listening, and acting on messages. How are each of these being demonstrated or amplified in you?

_____

_____

_____

_____

Chapter 38
Soul Inspired Action, Creation, and Healing

Describe an example of how Grace has been showered upon you.

_____

_____

_____

_____

_____

_____

_____

_____

_____

Chapter 38
Soul Inspired Action, Creation, and Healing

Chapter 38
Soul Inspired Action, Creation, and Healing

Chapter 38
Soul Inspired Action, Creation, and Healing

Superb job! Your experiences and stronger bonds with the Akashic Beings of Light have brought you uinto energetic unity with your Soul. Recognize your efforts and bravery in acquiring new skills. Have fun creating from this new vantage point! We will see you on the inner planes of your Soul. Always here for you.

— Akashic Beings of Light

Chapter 39
By the Power of Divine Light Within Me

How has the Divine utilized your flaws to good purpose?

_____

_____

_____

_____

How has the Divine used your mistakes to promote your spiritual growth?

_____

_____

_____

_____

"She is many steps ahead of you laying the groundwork of your path, while being uniquely in-step with you as you walk your path." What thoughts and feelings does this statement arouse?

_____

_____

_____

_____

Chapter 39
By the Power of Divine Light Within Me

Chapter 39
By the Power of Divine Light Within Me

Chapter 39
By the Power of Divine Light Within Me

Outstanding work! Your willingness to surrender combined with your new experiences have profoundly deepened connections with your Akashic Records, your spiritual guides, and have enriched your Soul Consciousness. Validate your efforts and sheer bravery in asking deep questions, receiving high level answers while learning new skills. We will meet you on your Soul's inner planes. Ever at your service.

— Akashic Beings of Light

Chapter 40
Final Messages

Chapter 40 of Bringing Forth Soul Consciousness, "Final Messages," offers concluding insights from the Akashic Beings of Light, the Great Creatress (the Divine) and the author. This chapter does not include interactive questions. Instead, it serves as a culmination of the wisdom imparted throughout the book, encouraging you to carry forward the teachings and continue your spiritual evolution with renewed clarity and purpose. It is an invitation to expand on what you have learned from this book.

Stay Connected

Thank you for embarking on this spiritual journey with me. It has been an honor to share the wisdom of the Akashic Records and the guidance of the Akashic Beings of Light. As you continue to explore and deepen your connection with your Soul, I invite you to stay connected with my work and the supportive community we've built.

This journal is the companion to my book, "**Bringing Forth Soul Consciousness**", which delves deeper into the practices, exercises, and teachings we have touched upon here in the journal. The book is designed to help you on your path to spiritual growth and enlightenment and is recommended to get the most out of the journal.

 Announcement: The audio version of my book "*Bringing Forth Soul Consciousness*" is now available! Find it at any of the these locations:

- Apple Books: AnnieChannels.com/audio-apple
- Storytel: AnnieChannels.com/audio-storytel
- Rakuten Kobo: AnnieChannels.com/audio-kobo
- Libro.FM: AnnieChannels.com/audio-libro
- Audio Books: AnnieChannels.com/audio-audiobooks
- Hoopla: AnnieChannels.com/audio-hoopla

Thank you for your commitment to your spiritual journey. I look forward to continuing this path together, sharing in the light and love of the Divine.

Find my latest book, teachings, events, offerings, and contact information on the following pages.

Love and Light,

Annie

205

Annie Bachelder on Facebook

Follow Reverend Annie Bachelder on Facebook to stay connected with her daily insights, live readings, and spiritual guidance. Annie's Facebook page is a hub of activity where she shares her wisdom and compassionate understanding to help you navigate your spiritual path with clarity and confidence. By following her, you'll gain access to exclusive content, be the first to know about upcoming events and special offers, and join a community of individuals dedicated to soul growth and healing. Annie's posts are designed to inspire, educate, and support you in your spiritual journey. Engage with her live sessions, where you can ask questions and receive real-time guidance. Join a nurturing community that values personal transformation and spiritual empowerment.

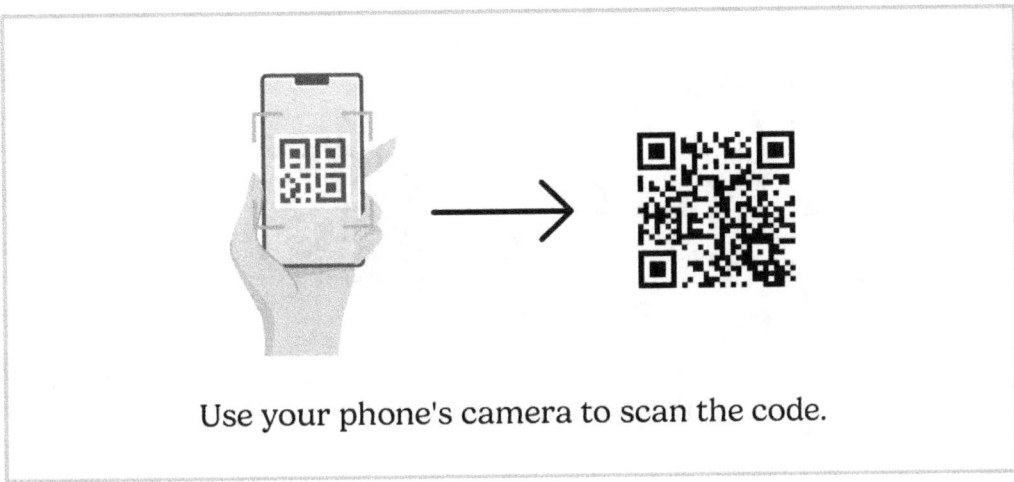

Use your phone's camera to scan the code.

Why follow Annie on Facebook?

- Get daily spiritual insights
- Join live readings and Q&A
- Access exclusive content and offers
- Stay updated on upcoming events
- Connect with a nurturing community

Bringing Forth Soul Consciousness Facebook Group

Join our vibrant Bringing Forth Soul Consciousness Facebook Group and connect with a community of like-minded souls who are passionate about soul consciousness. This private group is a sanctuary for those on their spiritual journey, offering a safe and supportive environment to share experiences, seek guidance, and find inspiration. Engage in meaningful conversations, participate in exclusive events, and access a wealth of resources that will support your growth and development. Our members are dedicated to uplifting each other, fostering a spirit of light and love, and creating a nurturing space for all. The BFSC Facebook Group is where you can connect deeply, share openly, and grow spiritually together.

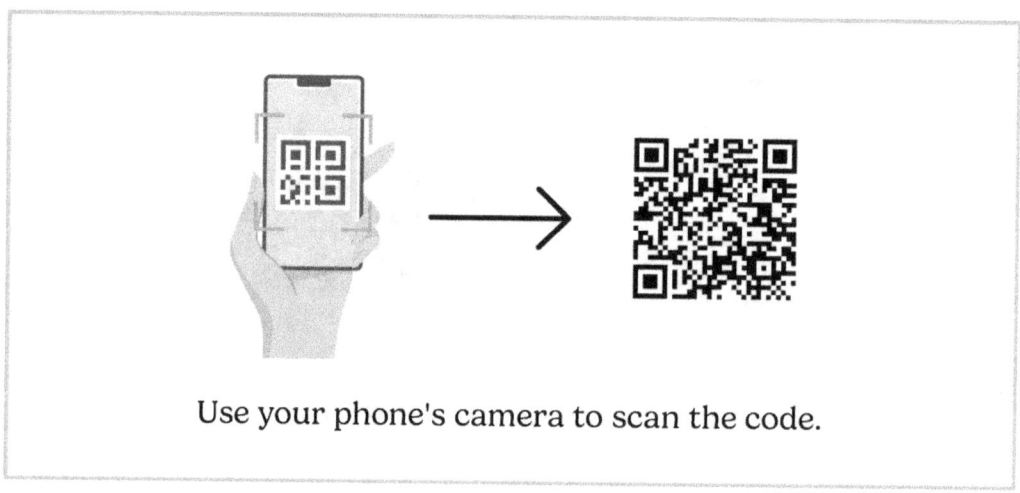

Use your phone's camera to scan the code.

Why join this exclusive Facebook group?

- Connect with like-minded souls
- Share your spiritual journey
- Participate in exclusive events
- Access a wealth of resources
- Engage in meaningful conversations

AnnieChannels.com Website

Visit AnnieChannels.com, your gateway to exploring the depths of your soul consciousness. This comprehensive website offers a treasure trove of resources tailored to support your spiritual journey. Discover a wide range of articles, videos, and tools designed to illuminate your path and provide practical guidance for your personal development. At AnnieChannels.com, you can book personal readings, access exclusive content, and explore various spiritual practices that resonate with your soul. The website is a reflection of Annie's deep commitment to helping others achieve spiritual enlightenment and growth. Whether you are seeking answers, looking for inspiration, or wanting to connect with a supportive community, AnnieChannels.com has everything you need.

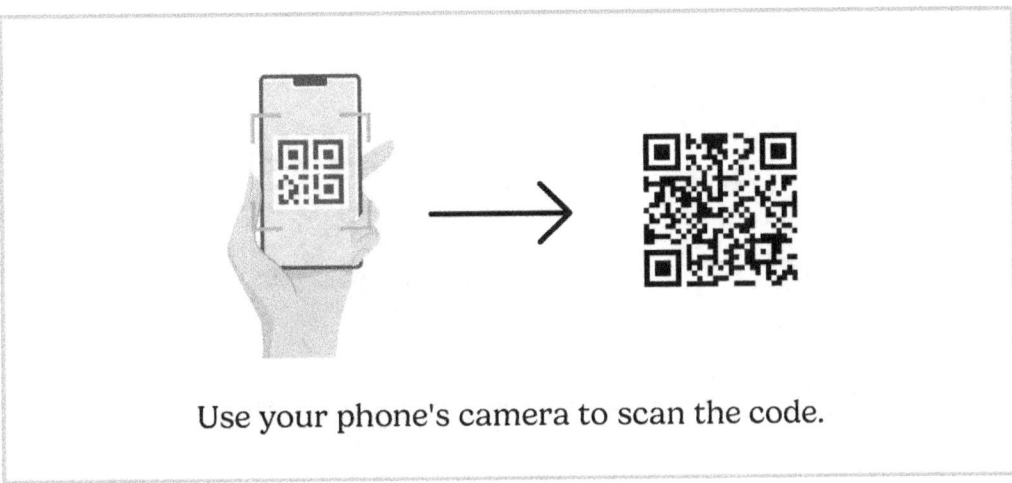

Use your phone's camera to scan the code.

Why visit AnnieChannels.com?

- Explore a bevy of spiritual resources
- Book personal readings with Annie
- Access exclusive articles and videos
- Discover practical spiritual tools
- Connect with a supportive community

Email Annie

Have questions or need personalized guidance? Email Annie directly for compassionate support and insightful readings tailored to your unique spiritual path. Annie is dedicated to providing you with the clarity and direction you need to navigate your soul's journey. Whether you are facing challenges, seeking deeper understanding, or looking for personal growth, her empathetic and intuitive approach will help illuminate your path. In your email, you can share your concerns, ask specific questions, or simply seek general guidance, and Annie will respond with thoughtful and personalized insights. Her responses are designed to provide you with the support and encouragement you need to move forward confidently.

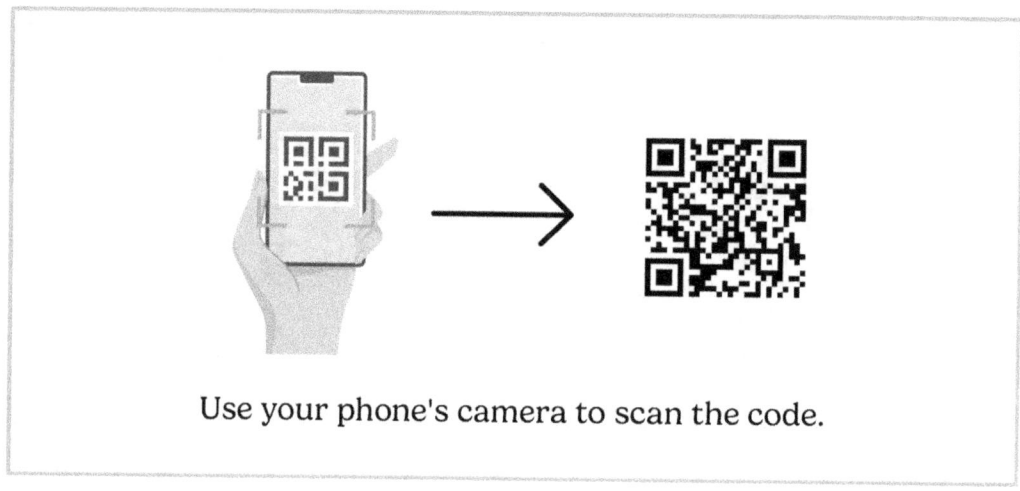

Use your phone's camera to scan the code.

Why email Annie?

- Receive personalized spiritual guidance
- Get compassionate support
- Ask specific questions and get tailored answers
- Share your concerns and challenges
- Gain clarity and direction for your journey

Phone Annie

For immediate and direct spiritual guidance, call Annie. Whether you need clarity, healing, or just a comforting voice, Annie is here to support you. Her empathetic and insightful approach can provide the answers and reassurance you need in moments of uncertainty. By speaking directly with Annie, you can receive personalized guidance tailored to your specific situation. Whether you're dealing with a pressing issue, seeking spiritual insight, or just need someone to talk to, Annie's compassionate support is just a phone call away. Feel empowered to reach out whenever you need assistance on your spiritual journey. Scan the QR code to call her and experience the guidance and support she offers firsthand.

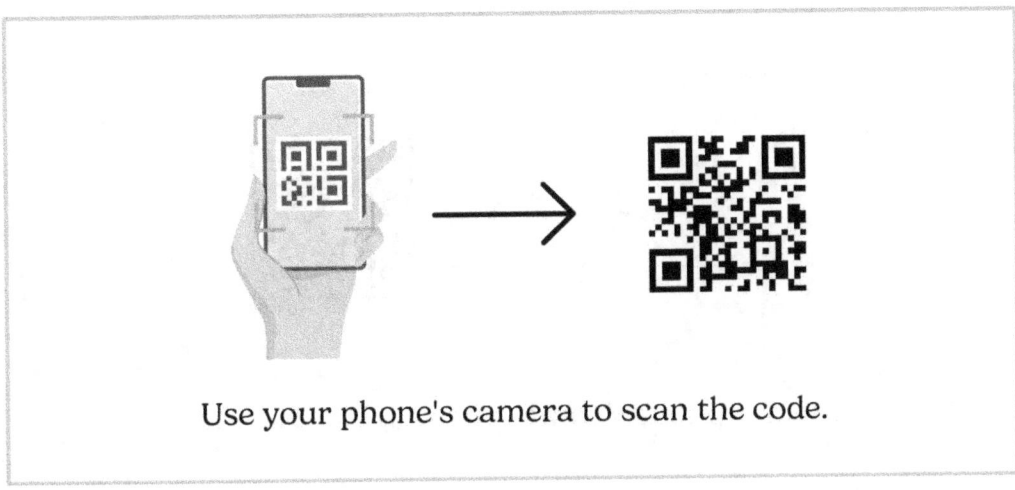

Use your phone's camera to scan the code.

Why phone Annie directly?

- Get immediate spiritual guidance
- Receive empathetic and insightful support
- Speak directly with Annie for personalized help
- Find reassurance in moments of uncertainty
- Empower yourself with direct spiritual insight

Annie on YouTube

Watch videos and subscribe to Annie Bachelder's YouTube channel for access to over 300 enlightening videos, guided meditations, and live channeling sessions. Annie's channel is a rich resource for anyone looking to deepen their understanding of soul consciousness and spiritual practices. Each video is carefully crafted to provide practical insights and spiritual knowledge that can help you on your journey. From exploring the mysteries of the soul to practical meditations that enhance your daily life, Annie's YouTube channel offers a wealth of information and inspiration. By subscribing, you'll be able to engage with new content regularly, participate in live sessions, and access a supportive community of like-minded individuals.

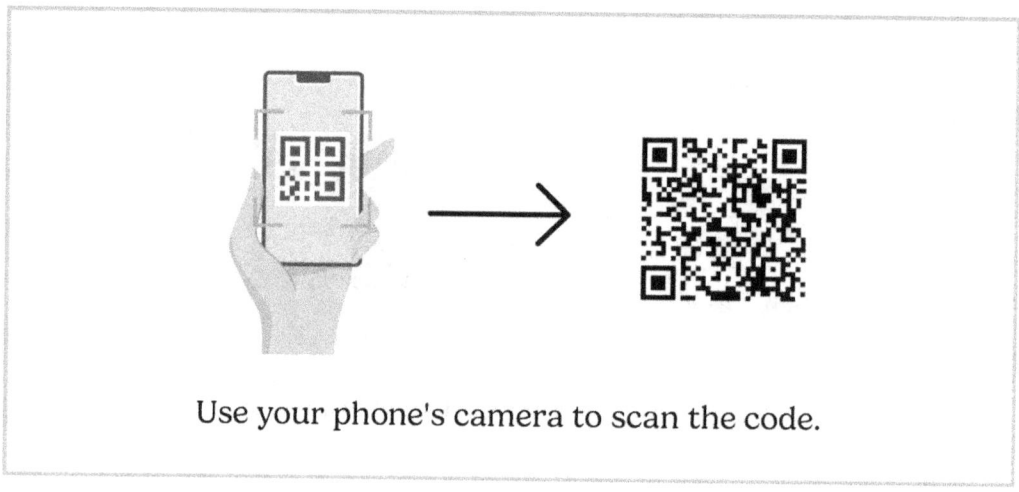

Use your phone's camera to scan the code.

Why visit Annie's YouTube channel?

- Access over 300 enlightening videos
- Join guided meditations and live sessions
- Deepen your understanding of spiritual practices
- Engage with a supportive community
- Stay inspired with regular new content

Amazon

Find Annie Bachelder's book and other products on Amazon to embark on a journey of self-discovery and soul empowerment. Her book is a beacon of light, offering profound insights and practical guidance to help you transform your life. Available in both Kindle and paperback formats, it provides an accessible and valuable resource for your spiritual journey. Annie's writing is designed to inspire, educate, and support you as you explore the depths of your soul consciousness. By reading her book, you can gain new perspectives, find answers to your questions, and receive the encouragement you need to pursue your spiritual path with confidence. Scan the QR code to purchase her book on Amazon and bring home a piece of wisdom that will illuminate your path and enrich your soul's growth.

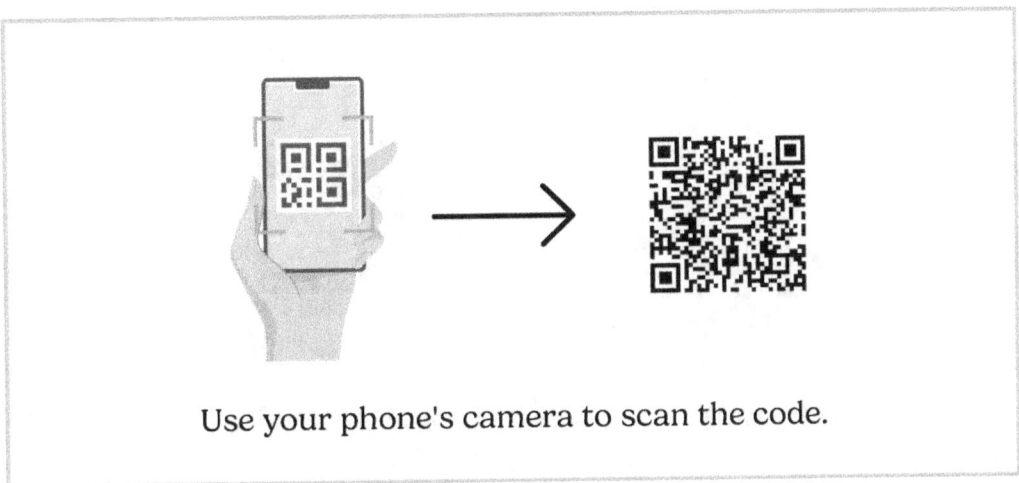

Use your phone's camera to scan the code.

Why check out Annie on Amazon?

- Purchase Annie Bachelder's book
- Available in Kindle and paperback
- Gain empowering spiritual insights
- Transform your life with practical guidance
- Illuminate your path with Annie's wisdom

Etsy

Explore Annie's Etsy shop "Soul Sourcer" for a range of spiritual resources designed to support your soul's journey. The shop features the companion journal digital download, book download, and various offerings that enhance your spiritual practice. These resources are designed to complement your reading and provide practical tools that you can integrate into your daily life. The companion journal offers a space for reflection and growth, while the book download provides convenient access to Annie's profound insights. Additionally, the shop includes downloadable printable individual chapters, prayers, affirmations, digital files for meditations, audio meditations, and audio chapters. Each item is crafted to support your spiritual growth.

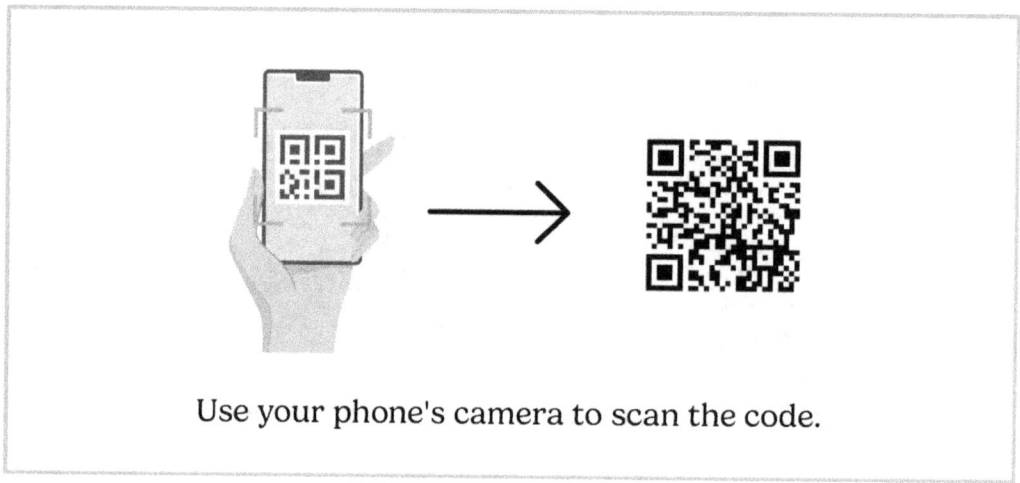

Use your phone's camera to scan the code.

What will you find in the "Soul Sourcer" Etsy shop?

- Download the companion journal
- Access Annie's book in digital format
- Find spiritual tools and resources
- Explore meditations and affirmations
- Enhance your spiritual practice

Glossary

Akashic Records: A metaphysical compendium of all universal events, including each Soul's every thought, word, emotion, and intention ever occurring in the past, present, and having the probability of occurring in the future. The Akashic Records are an energetic archive of the Soul's journey, accessible for guidance, healing, and spiritual growth.

Agape: Unconditional, selfless love that transcends the physical realm, representing spiritual ideals. It is the highest form of love, reflecting Divine love and compassion.

Anubis: An Egyptian deity associated with the afterlife and mummification, who weighed the human heart against a feather. Those who's hearts weighed less than a feather Anubis escorted to the afterlife. If not, they were required to live another life on earth. In our spiritual work, Anubis serves as a guardian and guide, assisting souls with higher information and energy required for assimilating into the higher dimensional realms.

Channeling: The practice of communicating with spiritual entities of higher consciousness. Channeling involves receiving and transmitting loving messages, wisdom, and guidance from kind and supportive non-physical sources.

Divine Light: A term referring to the pure, spiritual energy that emanates from the Divine. Divine Light provides guidance, healing, and enlightenment, illuminating the path of spiritual growth.

Duality: The existence of two fundamental aspects or opposites, such as male and female, light and dark, right and wrong that define human experience on Earth. Duality is a key concept in understanding the balance and interplay of different forces in the universe.

Embodying Your Soul's Light: The process of integrating the Soul's wisdom and energy into the physical body. This practice heals the sense of separation between the physical and spiritual realms and aligns one with their Divine purpose.

214

Fear Not, Judge Not, Resist Not: The three principles that govern the Akashic Records. These principles create an atmosphere of sacred safety, kindness, and respect, allowing for true healing and spiritual growth.

Great Creatress: A term referring to the Divine Feminine aspect of creation, emphasizing the nurturing and life-giving force of the universe. The Great Creatress embodies unconditional love, wisdom, and absolute creative power.

Higher Consciousness: An elevated state of awareness that transcends ordinary perception. Higher Consciousness is often associated with spiritual enlightenment and a deeper connection to the Divine.

Masters, Teachers, and Loved Ones (MTLOs): Spiritual entities or guides related to your Akashic Records that provide unconditional love, wisdom, support, and guidance. They assist you on your spiritual journey and help you heal the past so you recognize and act on your Soul's purposes.

Receiver The part of a telephone apparatus contained in the earpiece, in which electrical signals are converted into sounds. Or - a person who gets or accepts something that has been sent or given to them, as in a receiver of a gift.

Transponder A device for receiving a radio signal and automatically transmitting a different signal.

Transmitter A set of electrical equipment used to generate and transmit electromagnetic waves carrying messages or signals. Or - short for neurotransmitter.

Moral Agency: The capacity to make ethical decisions and act in accordance with one's moral principles. It involves the exercise of free will in alignment with spiritual values and divine guidance.

Non-Gender-Based Consciousness: A state of awareness that transcends traditional gender roles and identities, embracing a more holistic view of existence. It recognizes the spiritual essence beyond physical gender distinctions.

Philos: A form of love that denotes deep friendship and emotional connection. It bridges the gap between the spiritual and physical, fostering companionship and mutual support.

Quantum Physics: A field of science that explores the behavior of matter and energy at the smallest scales. Quantum physics often intersects with concepts of consciousness and spirituality, suggesting a deeper connection between mind and matter.

Self-Pollination: The process by which a single organism fertilizes itself, symbolizing self-sufficiency and the integration of dual aspects within one being. In spiritual terms, it represents the ability to generate and sustain one's own spiritual growth.

Soul Consciousness: Awareness and connection to one's Soul, including understanding one's divine purpose and higher self. Soul Consciousness involves living in alignment with the Soul's wisdom and guidance.

Soul Evolution Stages: The process of spiritual growth and development that a Soul undergoes through multiple lifetimes. Stages include learning, healing, and integrating experiences to achieve higher levels of consciousness, compassion, and oneness with the Divine.

Soul's Energetic Blueprint: The unique pattern of energy that defines a Soul's purpose, lessons, and path. This blueprint guides the Soul's evolution and interactions across lifetimes.

Spiritual Heart: The Heart of your Soul, beyond your personality or physical self, center of one's being where divine love and higher consciousness are experienced and expressed. It is the seat of the Soul's wisdom and the source of true spiritual connection.

Spiritual Theory of Everything Model (STOEM): A conceptual framework that integrates spirituality, mathematics, and cosmology to explain the interconnectedness of the cosmos.

I and My Soul Are One Affirmations

I and my Soul are One.

I and my Soul are inseparable.

I and my Soul belong together.

I and my Soul walk hand in hand on the path of enlightenment together.

I trust my inseparable Soul to love me no matter what transpires.

I trust my inseparable Soul to stand by me.

My Soul has never, and will never, reject me.

Consciously linked, my Soul and I are clearly directed to the highest and best outcomes for our mutual benefit.

My Soul and I safely grow, expand, and explore together.

My Soul is my best friend and the keeper of my innermost gifts, talents, and abilities.

My Soul assists me with solutions, insights, and inspiration.

My Soul never abandons me in times of trouble.

My Soul aids in my healing, maturation, and supplies the courage needed to progress on my path.

My Soul actively draws me toward uplifting opportunities and abundance.

The more I merge with my Soul the more healed and whole I am.

The more my Soul merges with me, the more we can accomplish together.

The more I identify as my Soul, the capabilities for achieving my aspirations increase.

The more I identify as my Soul, the fewer limitations, distractions, and obstacles I experience.

The more my Soul becomes my human identity, the more peace, inclusivity, and harmony I experience.

I now see through the loving eyes of my Soul.

I now experience through the expanded awareness of my Soul.

I now love with my Spiritual Heart, the heart of my Soul.

I now clearly hear and follow the wisdom and direction of my Soul.

I and my Soul are indivisible.

My Soul and I are One, we are One with the Great Creatress (the Divine).

Thank you, Soul. Thank you, Great Creatress.

Great Creatress Invocations

Oh, Great Creatress!

I invite your Divine and Holy Presence to flow through me now.

Opening my Spiritual Heart, I receive the fullness of your gifts.

Perpetually aligned in Divine partnership with you, I offer my mind, body and spirit in unity with Your Power and Purpose.

Surrendering all obstacles, Your pure Light flows gracefully through me.

Receiving your Divine instructions for this day, all thoughts, words, and deeds that most serve You arrive preformatted with Your impeccable timing, love, and strength of purpose.

Inspire me to proceed in the direction and manner that You prescribe.

Born of Your Divine Light, and filled with gratitude, your steady Presence gives me the energy, clarity and empowerment needed to fulfill Your Divine Plan.

Gratefully, I say And so it is, Dear Goddess! Amen!

Integrating Soul Prayer

For the highest good of all, Great Creatress,

please, open my Spiritual Heart to full vibrancy.

Awaken me to your Divine Design.

By the power of your Spirit within me, I presence my Soul.

Oversee my Soul and physical experience as we become One.

Safe in Your embrace, my Soul's Light fills me to the brim.

Recognizing my Soul's Divinity and partnership with You,

I open to receive Its beneficial influence.

Blending fully with my Soul, I am strengthened.

My Soul neither dominates nor condemns me.

Rather, my Soul embraces me kindly,

Guides me wisely,

Fills my heart with Its love,

Sweetens my thoughts, words, and deeds with compassion.

My Soul naturally forms my link with Thee, Great Creatress.

May all consciousness be of the Light.

And so, it is.

Amen

Bringing Forth Soul Consciousness
Opening Prayer

1) By the Power of Divine Light within me

2) Come Holy Spirit! Spirit of Light! Spirit of Truth!

3) For the highest good of all, throughout time, fill my heart with Divine Love as

4) I humbly ask permission to open the Divine Portal to the highest realm of the Akashic Records for (LEGAL NAME).

5) Akashic Beings of Light, guide me to the deepest Truth of my being, releasing any blocks & restrictions to my abundance & highest good.

6) Great Creatress, assist me to fully embody my Soul's Light, to fulfill my Soul's purposes, & to heal any accumulated karma.

7) Surround me with the enlightenment & wisdom of my Masters, Teachers, & Loved Ones.

8) Clearly direct my perspective & actions to those that manifest my Divine Plan.

(Repeat lines 5, 6, 7, & 8 two more times, then say line 9)

9) Free of all resistance, judgment, and fear, I am now filled with Divine Love & the Records are open.

Closing Prayer

Thanking the Great Creatress & Her Holy Spirit for Love, protection & healing received this day,

Thanking the Akashic Beings of Light for guidance,

Thanking the Masters, Teachers, & Loved Ones for wisdom & direction.

The Divine Portal & the Akashic Records are now closed.

Amen. Amen. Amen.